JOSEPH
and the Hebrews in Egypt

Contemporary Bible Series
JOSEPH and the Hebrews in Egypt
Published by
Scandinavia Publishing House 2010
Drejervej 15,3 DK-2400 Copenhagen NV,
Denmark
Tel. (45) 3531 0330 Fax (45) 3536 0334
E-mail: info@scanpublishing.dk
Web: www.scandinavia.dk

Text copyright
© Contemporary English Version
Illustrations copyright
© Gustavo Mazali
Design by Ben Alex
Printed in China
ISBN 978 87 7247 453 3

JOSEPH
and the Hebrews in Egypt

Contemporary English Version

scandinavia

Contents

Jacob Works for Laban

Genesis 29:1-14

As Jacob continued on his way to the east, he looked out in a field and saw a well where shepherds took their sheep for water. Jacob went over to the well and asked the shepherds, "Do you know Nahor's grandson Laban?" "Yes, we do," they replied, "and here comes his daughter Rachel with the sheep."

When Jacob saw Rachel, he kissed her and started crying because he was so happy. He told her that he was the son of her aunt Rebekah. She ran and told her father about him. As soon as Laban heard the news, he ran out to meet Jacob. Laban said, "You are my nephew. You are like one of my own family."

Jacob Marries Leah and Rachel

Genesis 29:15-30

After Jacob had been there for a month, Laban said to him, "You shouldn't have to work without pay. What do you want me to give you?" Laban had two daughters. Leah was older than Rachel, but her eyes didn't sparkle, while Rachel was beautiful and had a good figure. Since Jacob was in love with Rachel, he answered, "If you will let me marry Rachel, I'll work seven years for you."

Jacob worked seven years for Laban. But the time seemed like only a few days, because he loved Rachel so much.

Finally Jacob said to Laban, "The time is up, and I want to marry Rachel now!"

Laban gave a big feast and invited all their neighbors. But

that evening he brought Leah to marry Jacob. Jacob asked Laban, "Why did you do this to me? Didn't I work to get Rachel?" Laban replied, "In our country the older daughter must get married first. After you spend this week with Leah, you may also marry Rachel. But you will have to work for me another seven years."

So Jacob had to work another seven years for Laban.

Jacob Becomes Rich

Genesis 30:25-43

After Jacob's son Joseph was born, Jacob said to Laban, "Release me from our agreement and let me return to my own country. You know how hard I've worked for you, so let me take my wives and children and leave." But Laban told him, "If you really are my friend, stay on, and I'll pay whatever you ask." Jacob told him, "I don't want you to pay me anything. Just do one thing. Let me go through your flocks and herds and take the sheep and goats that are either spotted or speckled and the black lambs." "I agree to that," was Laban's response.

Jacob cut branches from some trees. He peeled off part of the bark and made the branches look spotted and speckled. Then he put the branches where the sheep and goats would see them while they were drinking from the water trough. When the stronger sheep were mating near the drinking place, Jacob made sure that the spotted branches

8

were there. Their young turned out to be spotted and speckled. But he would not put out the branches when the weaker animals were mating.

In this way, Jacob built up a flock of sheep for himself. He got all of the healthy animals, and Laban got what was left. Jacob soon became rich and successful. He owned many sheep, goats, camels, and donkeys, as well as a lot of slaves.

9

Jacob Runs Away

Genesis 31:1-21

Jacob heard that Laban's sons were complaining, saying, "Jacob is now a rich man, and he got everything he owns from our father." Jacob also noticed that Laban was not as friendly as he had been before.

One day the Lord said, "Jacob, go back to your relatives in the land of your ancestors, and I will bless you."

Jacob sent for Rachel and Leah to meet him in the field where he kept his sheep. He told them, "You know that I have worked hard for your father and that he keeps cheating me by changing my wages time after time. But God has protected me. When your father said the speckled sheep would be my wages, all of them were speckled. And when he said the spotted ones would be mine, all of them were

spotted. That's how God has taken sheep and goats from your father and given them to me. I dreamed God's angel came to me and said, 'Leave here right away and return to the land where you were born.'"

Rachel and Leah said to Jacob, "Do whatever God tells you to do."

Jacob, his wives, and his children got on camels and left for the home of his father Isaac in Canaan. Before Rachel left, she stole the household idols while Laban was out shearing his sheep. Jacob tricked Laban by not saying that he intended to leave. When Jacob crossed the Euphrates River and headed for the hill country of Gilead, he took with him everything he owned.

Laban Catches Up With Jacob

Genesis 31:22-42

Three days later Laban found out that Jacob had gone. Laban chased after Jacob for seven days before catching up with him. God appeared to Laban in a dream that night and warned, "Don't say a word to Jacob. Don't make a threat or a promise."

Jacob had set up camp in the hill country of Gilead. Laban went to Jacob and said, "You've tricked me and run off with my daughters like a kidnapper. I can understand why you were eager to return to your father, but why did you have to steal my idols?" Jacob answered, "I left secretly because I was afraid you would take your daughters from me by force. If you find that any one of us has taken your idols, I'll have that person killed." Jacob did not realize that Rachel had stolen the household idols.

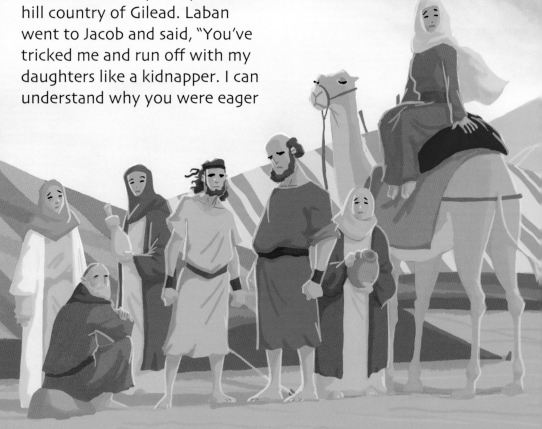

Laban searched the tents. Rachel had already hidden them in the cushion she used as a saddle and was sitting on it. Laban kept on searching but still did not find the idols. Jacob became very angry and said to Laban, "I had to work fourteen of these twenty long years to earn your two daughters and another six years to buy your sheep and goats. God saw my hard work, and he knew the trouble I was in, so he helped me. Then last night he told you how wrong you were."

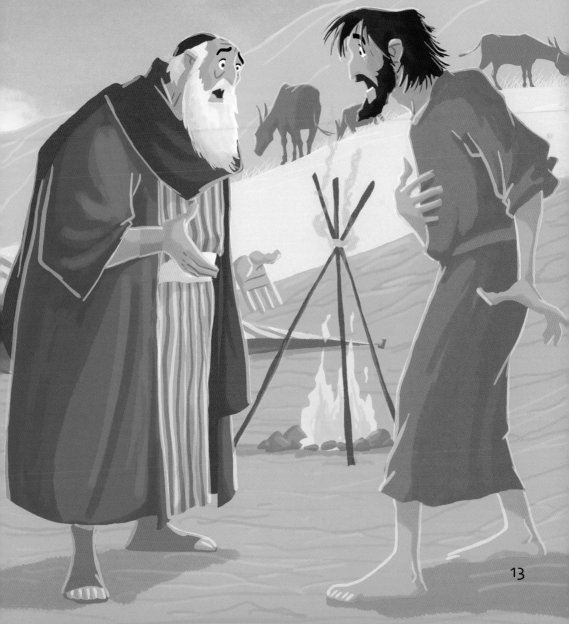

An Agreement is Made

Genesis 31:43-55

Laban said to Jacob, "There is nothing I can do to keep my daughters and their children. So I am ready to make an agreement with you. We will pile up some large rocks here to remind us that the Lord will watch us both while we are apart from each other."

Then Laban said, "If you mistreat my daughters or marry other women, I may not know about it, but remember, God is watching us! Both this pile of rocks and this large rock have been set up between us as a reminder. I must never go beyond them to attack you, and you must never go beyond them to attack me."

Then Jacob made a promise in the name of the fearsome God his father Isaac had worshiped. Jacob killed an animal and

offered it as a sacrifice there on the mountain, and he invited his men to eat with him. After the meal they spent the night on the mountain.

Early the next morning Laban kissed his daughters and his grandchildren goodbye. Then he left to go back home.

Jacob Gets Ready to Meet Esau

Genesis 32:1-21

As Jacob was on his way back home, he sent messengers on ahead to Esau. Esau lived in the land of Seir, also known as Edom. Jacob told his messengers to say to Esau, "Master, I am your servant! I am sending these messengers in the hope that you will be kind to me." When the messengers returned, they told Jacob, "We went to your brother Esau. He is heading this way with four hundred men."

Jacob was frightened. He divided his people, sheep, cattle, and camels into two groups. He thought, "If Esau attacks one group, perhaps the other can escape." Then Jacob prayed, "Please rescue me from my brother. I am afraid he will come and attack not only me, but my wives and children as well."

After Jacob had spent the night there, he chose some animals as gifts for Esau. Then he said to the servant in charge of the first herd, "When Esau meets you, tell him, 'They belong to your servant Jacob who is coming this way. He is sending them as a gift to his master Esau.'" Jacob also told the men in charge of the

16

second and third herds and those
who followed to say the same
thing when they met Esau.

Jacob hoped the gifts would
make Esau friendly. Jacob's men
took the gifts on ahead of him,
but he spent the night in camp.

Jacob Wrestles a Stranger

Genesis 32:22-32

Jacob got up in the middle of the night and took his wives, his eleven children, and everything he owned across to the other side of the Jabbok River for safety. Afterwards, Jacob went back and spent the rest of the night alone.

A man came and fought with Jacob until just before daybreak. When the man saw that he could not win, he struck Jacob on the hip and threw it out of joint. They kept on wrestling until the man said, "Let go of me! It's almost daylight."

"You can't go until you bless me," Jacob replied. Then the man asked, "What is your name?"

"Jacob," he answered. The man said, "Your name will no longer be Jacob. You have wrestled with God and with men, and you have won. That's why your name will be Israel." Jacob said, "Tell me your name." "Don't you know who I am?" he asked. And he blessed Jacob.

Jacob said, "I have seen God face to face, and I am still alive."

18

Jacob Meets Esau

Genesis 33: 1-17

Later that day Jacob met Esau coming with his four hundred men. So Jacob had his children walk with their mothers. Jacob himself walked in front of them all, bowing to the ground seven times as he came near his brother. Esau ran toward Jacob and hugged and kissed him. Then the two brothers started crying.

When Esau noticed the women and children he asked, "Whose children are these?" Jacob answered, "These are the ones the Lord has been kind enough to give to me, your servant."

Esau asked Jacob, "What did you mean by these herds I met along the road?" "Master," Jacob answered, "I sent them so that you would be friendly to me." "But, brother, I already have plenty," Esau replied. "Keep them for yourself."

"Let's get ready to travel," Esau said. "I'll go along with you." But Jacob answered, "Why don't you go on ahead and let me travel along slowly with the children, the herds, and the flocks. We can meet again in the country of Edom." Esau replied, "Let me leave some of my men with you."

"You don't have to do that," Jacob answered. "I am happy, simply knowing that you are friendly to me."

So Esau left for Edom. But Jacob went to Succoth, where he built a house for himself and set up shelters for his animals.

21

Joseph's Dream

Genesis 37:1-11

Jacob lived in the land of Canaan, where his father Isaac had lived. When Jacob's son Joseph was seventeen years old, he took care of the sheep with his brothers. Jacob had given Joseph a fancy coat to show that he was his favorite son. Joseph's brothers hated him and would not be friendly to him.

One day, Joseph told his brothers what he had dreamed. Joseph said, "Let me tell you about my dream. We were out in the field, tying up bundles of wheat. Suddenly my bundle stood up, and your bundles gathered around and bowed down to it." His brothers asked, "Do you really think you are going to be king and rule over us?" Now they hated Joseph more than ever because of what he had said about his dream.

Later, Joseph had another dream. He told his brothers, "Listen to what else I dreamed. The sun, the moon, and eleven stars bowed down to me." When he told his father about this dream, his father said, "What's that supposed to mean? Are

your mother and I and your brothers all going to come and bow down in front of you?"

Joseph's brothers were jealous of him, but his father kept wondering about the dream.

23

Joseph Is Thrown into a Well

Genesis 37:12-24

One day Joseph's brothers had taken the sheep to a pasture near Shechem.

Joseph's father said to him, "Go and find out how your brothers and the sheep are doing. Then come back and let me know." Joseph found his brothers in Dothan. But before he got there, they saw him coming and made plans to kill him.

They said to one another, "Look, here comes the hero of those dreams! Let's kill him and throw him into a pit and say that some wild animal ate him. Then we'll see what happens to those dreams." Reuben heard this and tried to protect Joseph from them. "Let's not kill him," he said. "Don't murder him or even harm him. Just throw him into a dry well out here in the desert." Reuben planned to rescue Joseph later and take him back to his father.

When Joseph came to his brothers, they pulled off his fancy coat and threw him into a dry well.

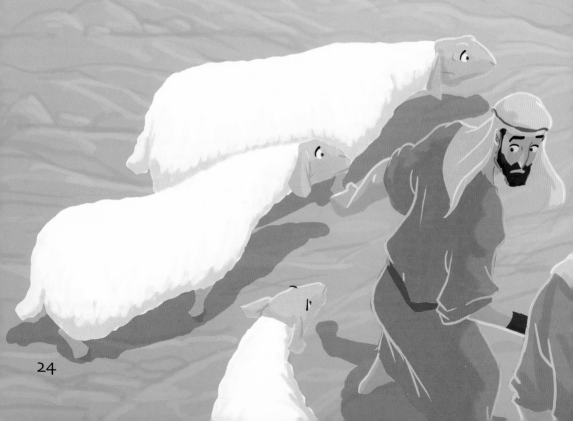

Joseph Is Taken to Egypt

Genesis 37:25-35

As Joseph's brothers sat down to eat, they looked up and saw a caravan of Ishmaelites coming from Gilead. Their camels were loaded with all kinds of spices that they were taking to Egypt. Judah said, "Let's sell Joseph to the Ishmaelites and not harm him. After all, he is our brother." The others agreed.

Joseph's brothers took him out of the well, and for twenty pieces of silver they sold him to the Ishmaelites who took him to Egypt.

Joseph's brothers killed a goat and dipped Joseph's fancy coat in its blood. After this, they took the coat to their father and said, "We found this! Look at it carefully and see if it belongs to your son." Jacob knew it was Joseph's coat and said, "It's my son's coat! Joseph has been torn to pieces and eaten by some wild animal."

Jacob mourned for Joseph a long time. To show his sorrow he tore his clothes and wore sackcloth. All of Jacobs's children came to comfort him, but he refused to be comforted. "No," he said, "I will go to my grave, mourning for my son." So Jacob kept on grieving.

In the House of Potiphar

Genesis 39:1-6

Meanwhile, the Ishmaelites took Joseph to Egypt and sold him to Potiphar. Potiphar was the king's official in charge of the palace guard. So Joseph lived in the home of Potiphar, his Egyptian owner. Soon Potiphar realized that the Lord was helping Joseph to be successful in whatever he did. Potiphar liked Joseph. He made him his personal assistant.

He put Joseph in charge of his house and all of his property. Because of Joseph, the Lord began to bless Potiphar's family and fields. He left everything up to Joseph. With Joseph there, the only decision Potiphar had to make was what he wanted to eat.

29

Joseph in Prison

Genesis 39:7-20

Joseph was well-built and handsome. Potiphar's wife soon noticed him. She asked him to make love to her, but he refused. He said, "No one in my master's house is more important than I am. The only thing he hasn't given me is you, and that's because you are his wife. I won't sin against God by doing such a terrible thing as this."

One day, Joseph went to Potiphar's house to do his work. Potiphar's wife grabbed hold of his coat and said, "Make love to me!" Joseph ran out of the house, leaving her hanging onto his coat. When this happened, she called in her servants and said, "Look! This Hebrew has come just to make fools of us. He tried to rape me. When he heard me scream, he ran out of the house, leaving his coat with me."

Potiphar's wife kept Joseph's coat until her husband came home. Then she said, "That Hebrew slave of yours tried to rape me!" Potiphar became very angry and threw Joseph in the same prison where the king's prisoners were kept.

Joseph Interprets Dreams

Genesis 40:1-23

While Joseph was in prison, both the king's personal servant, and his chief cook made the king angry. The king had them thrown into the same prison with Joseph.

One night each of the two men had a dream, but their dreams had different meanings. Joseph said to them, "Doesn't God know the meaning of dreams? Now tell me what you dreamed."

The king's personal servant told Joseph, "In my dream I saw a vine with three branches. As soon as it budded, I held the king's cup and squeezed the grapes into it. Then I gave the cup to the king." Joseph said, "This is the meaning of your dream. The three branches stand for three days, and in three days the king will pardon you. When these good things happen, please don't forget to tell the king about me, so I can get out of this place.

Then the chief cook told Joseph, "I also had a dream. In it I was carrying three breadbaskets stacked on top of my head. The top basket was full of all kinds of baked things for the king, but birds were pecking at them."

Joseph said, "This is the meaning of your dream. In three days the king will cut off your head. He will hang your body on a pole, and birds will come and peck at it."

Three days later everything happened just as Joseph had said it would. But the king's personal servant completely forgot about Joseph.

33

The King's Dreams

Genesis 41:1-32

Two years later, the king of Egypt had a dream. He dreamed that he was standing by the Nile River. Suddenly, seven fat, healthy cows came up from the river and started eating grass along the bank. Then seven ugly, skinny cows came up out of the river and ate the fat, healthy cows. When this happened, the king woke up. The king went back to sleep and had another dream. This time, seven full heads of grain were growing on a single stalk. Then seven other heads of grain appeared, but they were thin and scorched by the east wind. The thin heads of grain swallowed the seven full heads.

The next morning the king was upset. He called in his magicians and wise men and told them what he had dreamed. None of them could tell him what the dreams meant. The king's personal servant said, "Now I remember what I was supposed to do. When you were angry with me and your chief cook, you threw us both in jail. One night we both had dreams, and each dream had a different meaning. A young Hebrew, who was a servant of the captain of the guard, was there with us at the time. When we told him our dreams, he explained what each of them meant, and everything happened just as he said it would."

34

The king sent for Joseph, who was quickly brought out of jail. He shaved, changed his clothes, and went to the king. The king said to him, "I am told that you can interpret dreams." "Your Majesty," Joseph answered, "I can't do it myself, but God can give a good meaning to your dreams." Then the king told Joseph his dreams.

Joseph replied, "Your Majesty, both of your dreams mean the same thing, and in them God has shown what he is going to do. The seven good cows stand for seven years and so do the seven good heads of grain. The dreams mean there will be seven years when there won't be enough grain. The good years of plenty will be forgotten. Everywhere in Egypt people will be starving."

Joseph Is Made Governor over Egypt

Genesis 41:33-46

Joseph said, "Your Majesty, you should find someone who is wise

and will know what to do so that you can put him in charge of all Egypt. Then appoint some other officials to collect one-fifth of every crop harvested in Egypt during the seven years when there is plenty. It can be stored until it is needed during the seven years when there won't be enough grain in Egypt."

The king and his officials liked this plan. So the king said to them, "No one could possibly handle this better than Joseph, since the Spirit of God is with him." Then the king took off his royal ring and put it on Joseph's finger. He gave him fine clothes to wear and placed a gold chain around his neck. He also let him ride in the chariot next to his own.

People shouted, "Make way for Joseph!" So Joseph was governor of Egypt.

Seven Years of Famine

Genesis 41:47-57

Joseph was thirty when the king made him governor. He went everywhere for the king. For seven years there were big harvests of grain. Joseph collected and stored up the extra grain in the cities of Egypt near the fields where it was harvested. In fact, there was so much

grain that they stopped keeping record. It was like counting the grains of sand along the beach.

Egypt's seven years of plenty came to an end. The seven years of famine began, just as Joseph had said. There was not enough food in other countries, but all over Egypt there was plenty. When the famine finally struck Egypt, the people asked the king for food. The king said, "Go to Joseph and do what he tells you to do." The famine became bad everywhere in Egypt.

So Joseph opened the storehouses and sold the grain to the Egyptians. People from all over the world came to Egypt because the famine was severe in their countries.

Joseph's Brothers Go to Egypt

Genesis 42:1-24

When Jacob found out there was grain in Egypt, he said to his sons, "I have heard there is grain in Egypt. Go down and buy some, so we won't starve to death." Ten of Joseph's brothers went to Egypt to buy grain. But Jacob did not send Joseph's younger brother Benjamin with them. He was afraid that something might happen to him. Since Joseph was governor of Egypt and in charge of selling grain, his brothers came to him and bowed with their faces to the ground. They did not recognize Joseph. But right away he knew who they were, though he pretended not to know.

He asked, "Where do you come from?" "From the land of Canaan," they answered. "We've come here to buy grain. We come from a family of twelve brothers. The youngest is still with our father in Canaan, and one of our brothers is dead." Joseph remembered what he had dreamed about them and said, "You're spies! Since I respect God, I'll give you a chance to save your lives. If you are honest men, one of you must stay here in jail, and the rest of you can take the grain back to your starving families. But you must bring your youngest brother to me. Then I'll know that you are telling the truth, and you won't be put to death."

Joseph's brothers agreed and said to one another, "We're being

punished because of Joseph. We saw the trouble he was in, but we refused to help him when he begged us. That's why these terrible things are happening." Reuben spoke up, "Didn't I tell you not to harm the boy? But you wouldn't listen, and now we have to pay the price for killing him." They did not know that Joseph could understand them, since he was speaking through an interpreter. Joseph turned away from them and cried, but soon he turned back and spoke to them again.

Then he had Simeon tied up and taken away while they watched.

41

Joseph's Brothers Return to Canaan

Genesis 42:25-38

Joseph gave orders for his brothers' grain sacks to be filled with grain and for their money to be put in their sacks. When they stopped for the night, one of them opened his sack to get some grain for his donkey, and right away he saw his moneybag. "Here's my money!" he told his brothers. "Right here in my sack."

They were trembling with fear as they stared at one another and asked themselves, "What has God done to us?"

When they returned to the land of Canaan, they told their father Jacob everything that had happened to them. Jacob

said, "You have already taken my sons Joseph and Simeon from me. And now you want to take away Benjamin!" Reuben spoke up, "Father, if I don't bring Benjamin back, you can kill both of my sons. Trust me with him, and I will bring him back." But Jacob said, "I won't let my son Benjamin go down to Egypt with the rest of you. I am an old man, and if anything happens to him on the way, I'll die from sorrow."

Jacob Lets Benjamin Go

Genesis 43: 1-23

The famine in Canaan got worse. Jacob's family had eaten all the grain they had bought in Egypt. So Jacob said to his sons, "Go back and buy some more grain." Judah replied, "If you let us take Benjamin along, we will go and buy grain. But we won't go without him!"

Their father said, "If Benjamin must go with you, take the governor a gift of some of the best things from our own country, such as perfume, honey, spices, pistachio nuts, and almonds. Also take along twice the amount of money for the grain. There must have been some mistake when the money was put back in your sacks."

When they arrived at Joseph's house, they said to the servant in charge, "Sir, we came to Egypt once before to buy grain. But when we stopped for the night,

we each found in our grain sacks
the exact amount we had paid.
We have brought that money
back. We don't know who put
the money in our sacks."

"It's all right," the servant
replied. "The God you and your
father worship must have put
the money there. I received
your payment in full." Then he
brought Simeon out to them.

45

Joseph and Benjamin
Genesis 43:24-34

The servant took them into Joseph's house and gave them water to wash their feet. He also tended their donkeys. When Joseph came home, they gave him the gifts they had brought, and they bowed down to him. After Joseph had asked how they were, he said, "What about your elderly father? Is he still alive?" They answered, "Your servant our father is still alive and well." And again they bowed down to Joseph.

When Joseph looked around and saw his brother Benjamin, he said, "This must be your youngest brother, the one you told me about. God bless you, my son." Right away he rushed off to his room and cried because of his love for Benjamin. After washing his face and returning, he said, "Serve the meal!"

To the surprise of Joseph's brothers, they were seated in front of him according to their ages, from the oldest to the youngest. They were served food

46

from Joseph's table. Benjamin was given five times as much as each of the others. Joseph's brothers drank with him and had a good time.

The Stolen Cup

Genesis 44:1-17

Later, Joseph told the servant in charge of his house, "Fill the men's grain sacks with as much as they can hold and put their money in the sacks. Also put my silver cup in the sack of the youngest brother." Early the next morning, the men were sent on their way with their donkeys. But they had not gone far from the city when Joseph told the servant, "Go after those men! When you catch them, say, 'My master has been good to you. So why have you stolen his silver cup?'"

When the servant caught up with them, he said exactly what Joseph had told him to say.

But they replied, "Sir, we would never do anything like that! If you find that one of us has the cup, then kill him. The rest of us will become your slaves." Each of the brothers quickly put his sack on the ground and opened it. Joseph's servant started searching the sacks, beginning with the one that belonged to the oldest brother.

When he came to Benjamin's sack, he found the cup. This upset the brothers so much that they began tearing their clothes in sorrow. Then they loaded their donkeys and returned to the city. Joseph told them, "I would never punish all of you. Only the one who was caught with the cup will become my slave. The rest of you are free to go home to your father."

48

Judah Pleads for Benjamin

Genesis 44:14-34

Judah went over to Joseph and said, "Sir, you have as much power as the king himself. I am only your slave. Please don't get angry if I speak. You asked us if our father was still alive and if we had any more brothers. Our father's favorite wife had given birth to two sons. One of them was already missing and had not been seen for a long time. My father thinks the boy was torn to pieces by some wild animal. Now Benjamin is the only one of the two brothers who is still alive, and our father loves him very much.

"I promised my father that I would bring him safely home. Sir, I am your slave. Please let me stay here in place of Benjamin and let him return home with his brothers. How can I face my father if Benjamin isn't with me? I couldn't bear to see my father in such sorrow."

51

Joseph Tells the Truth

Genesis 45:1-15

Since Joseph could no longer control his feelings in front of his servants, he sent them out of the room. Joseph asked his brothers if his father was still alive, but they were too frightened to answer. Joseph told his brothers to come closer to him.

Then he said, "I am your brother Joseph, the one you sold into Egypt. Don't worry or blame yourselves for what you did. God is the one who sent me ahead of you to save lives. There has already been a famine for two years. For five more years no one will plow fields or harvest grain. But God sent me on ahead of you to keep your families alive and

to save you in this wonderful way. After all, you weren't really the ones who sent me here, it was God. Now tell my father that his son Joseph says, 'God has made me ruler of Egypt.' Tell my father about my great power here in Egypt and about everything you have seen. Hurry and bring him here."

Joseph and Benjamin hugged each other and started crying. Joseph was still crying as he kissed each of his other brothers.

The King Welcomes Joseph's Family

Genesis 45:16-28

When it was told in the palace that Joseph's brothers had come, the king and his officials were happy. The king said to Joseph, "Tell your brothers to load their donkeys and return to Canaan. Tell them to take some wagons from Egypt for their wives and children to ride in. And be sure to have them bring their father. They can leave their possessions behind because they will be given the best of everything in Egypt."

Joseph's brothers left Egypt. When they arrived in Canaan, they told their father that Joseph was still alive and was the ruler of Egypt. But their father was so surprised that he could not believe them. Then they told him everything Joseph had said. When he saw the wagons Joseph had sent, he felt much better and said, "Now I can believe you! My son Joseph must really be alive. I will get to see him before I die."

Joseph's Family Settles in Egypt

Genesis 47:1-12

Joseph took five of his brothers to the king and told him, "My father and my brothers have come from Canaan." The king asked Joseph's brothers, "What do you do for a living?"

"Sir, we are shepherds," was their answer. "Our families have always raised sheep. But in our country all the pastures are dried up, and our sheep have no grass to eat." The king said to Joseph, "It's good that your father and brothers have arrived. I will let them live anywhere they choose in the land of Egypt, but I suggest that they settle in Goshen, the best part of our land. I would also like for your finest shepherds to watch after my own sheep and goats."

Then Joseph brought his father Jacob to the king. The king asked him, "How old are you?" Jacob answered, "I have lived only a hundred thirty years, and I have had to move from place to place. My parents and my grandparents also had to move from place to place. But they lived much longer, and their life was not as hard as mine." Then Jacob gave the king his blessing.

Joseph obeyed the king's orders and gave his father and brothers some of the best land in Egypt.

Jacob Blesses Joseph's Two Sons

Genesis 48:1-2; 8-22

Joseph was told that his father Jacob had become very sick. Joseph went to see him and took along his two sons, Manasseh and Ephraim. Jacob was very old and almost blind. He did not recognize the two boys. He asked Joseph, "Who are these boys?" Joseph answered, "They are my sons. God has given them to me here in Egypt." "Bring them to me," Jacob said. "I want to give them my blessing."

Joseph led his younger son Ephraim to the left side of Jacob and his older son Manasseh to the right. But before Jacob gave them his blessing, he crossed his arms, putting his right hand on the head of Ephraim and his left hand on the head of Manasseh. Joseph did not like it when he saw his father place his right hand on the head of the younger son. Joseph said, "Father, you have made a mistake. This is the older boy. Put your right hand on him."

His father said, "Son, I know what I am doing. It's true that Manasseh's family will someday become a great nation. But Ephraim will be even greater than Manasseh, because his descendants will become many great nations."

After that, Jacob said, "Joseph, you can see that I won't live much longer. But God will be with you and will lead you back to the land he promised our family long ago. Meanwhile, I'm giving you the hillside I captured from the Amorites."

Joseph's Promise

Genesis 50: 15-21

After Jacob died, Joseph's brothers said to each other, "What if Joseph still hates us and wants to get even with us for all the cruel things we did to him?" They sent this message to Joseph: "Before our father died, he told us, 'You did some cruel and terrible things to Joseph. You must ask him to forgive you.' We ask you to please forgive the terrible things we did. After all, we serve the same God that your father worshiped."

When Joseph heard this, he started crying. Right then, Joseph's brothers came and bowed down to the ground in front of him and said, "We are your slaves." Joseph told them, "Don't be afraid! I have no right to change what God has decided. You tried to harm me, but God made it turn out for the best,

so that he could save all these people, as he is now doing. Don't be afraid! I will take care of you and your children."

After Joseph said this, his brothers felt much better.